PRAISE FOR
The Shrink Has Shrunk

"Writing not only for the healthcare provider but also the healthcare consumer, Dr. John Ruggiano displays a sophisticated understanding of changes in psychiatric medicine over time, writing as well as he thinks. Eye-opening and thought provoking, this book is a must read."

Tara Scungio PMHNPBC, LICSW

"Dr. Ruggiano discusses the experiences he has had in his career and the changes he has witnessed in identifying and treating behavioral health issues. He does so with a relatable and easy to understand narrative that resonates with those working in or impacted by the mental health field."

Joan Petrucci Andrews Ed.D, LMHC

ALSO BY JOHN RUGGIANO

Be Americanized

The Shrink Has Shrunk

I've Lost My Identity as a Psychiatrist

John Ruggiano

Copyright © 2023 by John Ruggiano

All rights reserved. This book or any portion thereof may not be reproduced or used in any manner whatsoever without the express written permission of the author except for the use of brief quotations in a book review.

Printed in the United States of America

First Printing, 2023

ISBN 979-8-218-27463-4

Photograph provided by the author

Designed by Randy Walters

Dedication

To Harry Stack Sullivan …

the person who was the biggest influence on my identity as a psychiatrist.

TABLE OF CONTENTS

The Title, Explained *1*

Introduction *3*

I Enter the Field of Psychiatry *5*

Relationships and the Interpersonal Method *7*

The Sullivan Method *9*

Big Changes *13*

The Medical Model *15*

The Medical Model, Continued *17*

Making a Diagnosis *19*

The DSM *23*

The Patients *25*

Addiction *29*

Lonely or Depressed *33*

The Approach-Avoidance Conflict *37*

The Histrionic Personality *41*

Sleep *45*

More on Changes *49*

I Use the New Model *53*

Saying Goodbye *57*

The End *61*

Citations *xx*

About the Author *xx*

ACKNOWLEDGMENTS

*Thanks to Dr. Ed Iannuccilli and Randy Walters
for sharing their expertise, unending patience, and inspiration
through the completion of my books.*

THE TITLE, EXPLAINED

Before I get started with this story, I feel the need to explain the title. The title refers to the changes I have experienced in my fifty years in the practice of psychiatry. Fifty years ago, a psychiatrist was responsible for treating people. We had to address the problems of the "whole person." That meant a consideration and discussions with the patient about their symptoms, what illness might be causing those symptoms, and how those symptoms were impacting the patient's function at work and in relationships.

Now our task is a focus on what brain chemistry we can change with a medication. The people we used to treat are now treated by counselors, nurse practitioners, primary care physicians, and sometimes a neurologist. I'm now left to wonder if I am even needed anymore. If that team of mental health workers just mentioned is not enough to get rid of me, an even greater threat to my worth is the internet!

In the place on my office wall where one would expect to see a diploma or certificate of accomplishment, I have a sign that reads: *Don't confuse your Google search with my medical degree.* In spite of that, most patients continue to tell me what I should be prescribing.

Yes, I am shrinking.

INTRODUCTION

I have been in the practice of psychiatry for fifty years; fifty years of experiencing and witnessing the marvels of the human brain and what that magnificent organ produces in the form of behaviors, creations, and sometimes crazy ideas.

I have seen extraordinarily successful people in business fail miserably in their family lives. They are leaders in their field, admired by their competitors, and respected by their employees, but have no meaningful, lasting relationships. There is also the inverse ... people who fail vocationally, can never get anything right at their job, but are loved by their children and welcomed by a large circle of friends. Some of the people in these examples have benefited by my care. Yet many have wasted their time in therapy and then blame everyone in their lives for their failures.

What follows is a recounting of those experiences in memoir rather than textbook form. I will share memories of fascinating people and their adventures.

I have tried to connect those people and their behaviors to the science that is supposed to explain those behaviors. I have rarely been able to do that. That is to say, there are textbooks and literature that are supposed to classify people into diagnostic categories with predictable courses of behavior. The textbooks and research of patients promise to predict outcomes and responses to treatments. That hasn't been my experience. My experiences and memories of those patients have not easily fit into those textbook descriptions. You may be surprised to read that my patients, as you will see, have never fit neatly into any diagnosis and certainly have never had a predictable response to treatment.

It will very soon become apparent that this book is not a text of science. There are no scientifically proven data. References at the end of each chapter are scarce or absent. There are no studies here in which groups of patients treated with a medication are compared with those treated with a placebo. The scientists call these studies "double-blind, placebo-controlled studies." Instead the reader will see an array of many opinions, observations, recollections, and ironies collected by me over the fifty year experience of my practice of psychiatry. It is a narrative of personal experience.

I will refer to many authors and practitioners, but the references are from memory, and so are not listed in a bibliography or reference list. Memories tend to get distorted over time. That may not be a loss though, for the distortion may be another new and useful idea. I realized this when I tried to explain some of the ideas of Harry Stack Sullivan. I have been teaching his interpersonal method of therapy based on my memory of his work that I read forty years ago. In a recent review of his work, I see that I have distorted some of his ideas into my own method.

I would like to think that the distortions of his method are more of an adaptation or possibly a refinement needed for the changes in our culture. In his day Sullivan may have had to deal with patients who were struggling with sexual conflicts. Today, dependence and aggression in interpersonal relationships constitute more of what my patients have presented. The result is that even though the subjects and conflicts dealt with in therapy have changed, the process of the therapeutic relationship that I have used is still based on Sullivan's work.

CHAPTER I

I ENTER THE FIELD OF PSYCHIATRY

It was 1959, my first year of college and in Psychology 101, I became fascinated with the concepts of Freud. At that time, Freud defined psychiatry, and I was intrigued by such thoughts as sexual repression, libido, conflicts of id and superego.

Then in 1970, my first year of psychiatric residency training, Freud was history. There was no mention of him in lectures and meetings. Psychopharmacology was now the focus of attention of every psychiatrist and every student in the field of psychiatry. All the journals and publications of psychiatry dealt almost exclusively with pharmacology. Journals such as *Psychiatric Annals* or *Current Psychiatry* were filled with "double-blind, placebo-controlled studies." Those consisted of groups of patients treated with drugs compared to patients treated with a placebo. Conferences and even lunch time banter was focused on Thorazine, Elavil and then a never-ending addition of new and supposedly more effective drugs.

I had a problem with this. Sure, pharmacology was often helpful, but my patients were presenting relationship problems … marital conflicts, workplace stress, identity confusion. Medication didn't help those problems very much. To my relief, I discovered Harry Stack Sullivan.

Sullivan was a student of Sigmund Freud and is often described in textbooks as a "Neo-Freudian." His method is called "Interpersonal Psychiatry," because the focus of his efforts centered on relationships. In my first years of the practice of psychiatry, I saw the need to address the problems of relationships that my patients were presenting. I began to define myself as an interpersonal counseling specialist and used the approach of Sullivan. It was a useful, effective method and I saw many people benefit from it.

Then recently, when the agency I work for asked me to instruct counselors in my method, I needed to return to the books on Sullivan. In refreshing my understanding of his method, I realized that over the years I had altered many of Sullivan's practices and added many of my own ideas. Comparing my mode of psychotherapy with the writings of Harry Stack Sullivan, I began to wonder if I should rename my method and call it Relationship Therapy. What follows is an explanation of a variation of "Interpersonal Psychiatry."

CHAPTER II

RELATIONSHIPS AND THE INTERPERSONAL METHOD

In college Physics 101 I discovered the interesting work of Isaac Newton. He believed that all objects in the universe were attracted to each other by a factor of their mass. He was sitting under an apple tree and saw that when an apple became ripe and its stem withered, it was pulled to the ground. He wondered why it didn't go up and then wondered why all objects not held up fell to the ground. He defined gravity.

I found that very interesting but over the years in my practice of psychiatry I began to think of an expansion or correlation of that idea.

My belief, method and approach to psychiatry became the idea that all people are attracted to each other. Certainly not by a factor of their mass. The factor that drew people to each other was determined by the absence of psychopathology. That is, the less psychopathology they are troubled with, the more they will feel a natural attraction to each other by a force akin to gravity. The attraction is not so much gravity as it is a human need for closeness, love, and contact.

My belief is that among humans there is a natural evolution of caring and trust that draws people together unless some form of pathology blocks that evolution.

I wonder how Newton would react to this addition, or variation of his brilliant ideas of gravity to a force that naturally pulls people together. I hope he wouldn't laugh at it. But on second thought maybe he should, because it is a rather funny extension of his thinking. I wish I could talk to him about it.

So whether it is a patient sitting with me in therapy, two co-workers at desks near each other, a teacher with a student, or even a waiter with a steady customer, there will be a gradual and natural growth of a relationship; an evolution of caring and trust. But that natural process won't happen if some symptom or psychologic problem gets in the way.

I saw an example of this even on my train commute to Boston two or three days a week for some consulting that I did. I noticed the same people sitting with each other every day, in groups. They sought each other out to laugh and joke about sports and the news or other topics. Some though, always sat alone and they would always be at a distance from the groups. My thought was that the people in the groups were the ones not troubled by psychopathology and without that obstacle, the natural, gravity like, evolution of caring and trust would occur.

These ideas about gravity related to human nature became poignant as I began to practice psychiatry. I saw patients struggling with relationship problems. Many were seeking trust and closeness and love but that "gravity" was blocked by various forms of mental and character traits called psychopathology.

In this context, early in my career of psychiatry I saw that this idea of a sort of gravity between people fit nicely into the concepts and methods of Harry Stack Sullivan, and his method of treatment called "Interpersonal Psychiatry." His ideas and method of helping people reinforced all my thinking about applying the concept of gravity to the natural draw or attraction of people to each other.

CHAPTER III

THE SULLIVAN METHOD

In the Sullivan method, the doctor-patient relationship was seen in what he called a "participant observation." This technique encouraged the patient to feel he had a partner to help him understand his problems. Sullivan was trained in the Freudian method of psychoanalysis. In that method the patient lay on a couch and was encouraged to do what Freud called "free association." This meant that the patient would recall his early life experiences. The patient developed a lot of insight. Sullivan saw that patients who were treated by this method became very much aware of how their problems developed. He also saw that some of them got better, but others didn't. He wondered what the curative factor was. He then saw that the more of a relationship the patient had with him, the more likely a change and improvement of problems would occur.

With this realization, Sullivan got rid of the couch and set two chairs at a forty-five degree angle so that doctor and patient could work as a team to understand the patient's problem. The patient then had a partner. The subject of discussion would be the relationship the patient had with other significant people in his developmental years. While the patient talked with his "partner" about his problems and their origins, a relationship developed with the psychiatrist. This relationship was in Sullivan's words, "corrective." He provided a "corrective emotional experience" which meant that the patient learned to relate to another person in a manner different from how they related to people in their early life.

An example of this would be seen in a person who grew up with an abusive father. That person would tend to relate to authority figures with an expectation of abuse. That expectation would block the natural evolution of caring and trust that should develop between any two people. Sullivan gave that person the experience of relating to an authority who could be trusted. This allowed the patient the new and corrective experience of sharing trust and caring in a relationship. Once the patient experienced this in his relationship with the therapist, he was then equipped and eager to experience it with others in his life.

Over the years of using this method, I began to focus more on the relationship the patient was developing with me, or more importantly, a focus on what was getting in the way of allowing the natural evolution of caring and trust.

I began to think of the therapy process in the Isaac Newton frame. Newton saw that all objects in the universe were attracted to each other with a force gravity. In humans the force would be a need for caring and trust. However, the patient would need to overcome pathology in order to allow that natural evolution to happen. That is where I came into the process. I saw my task as the need to identify and then encourage the removal of the pathology – the obstacle – so that the patient could experience healthy relationships.

My method would work in three stages.

Stage one: Identify the obstacles to the natural evolution of caring and trust that should develop between two people. These obstacles could be defenses such as paranoia, or avoidance for fear of failure. In my experience, the most common obstacle has been fear of rejection. It is ironic how many times I have seen people who will work hard to block the development of a relationship in order to protect themselves from the hurt of being rejected. But the result of their protective measures is rejection!

Stage two involves providing the patient with a "corrective emotional experience."

This happens when the patient begins to relate to me according to who I am rather than the hurtful and damaging person or people in his life. It corrects the tendency we all have to relate to new people with the "baggage" we carry from past relationships. Another part of this stage is that the patient begins to see themselves through my eyes instead of the eyes of some abusive parent or other important person in their life. Seeing ourselves through the eyes of parents as we grow up must have a lot to do with what identity we form.

I wish I could remember where I heard someone say, "I wish I were the man my dog sees." His dog, I'm sure, saw the greatest person in the world. That person with the terrible self image would not be such if his mother wagged her tail and snuggled up lovingly with him every time she saw him.

The "corrective" experience of stage two can happen even though I don't have a tail to wag. All it takes is some trust on the part of the patient to allow that natural caring to develop.

After the patient has had the experience of allowing a relationship to develop in treatment without their usual defenses or without their usual obstacle, they are ready to end a relationship in a healthy way. This is often an entirely new experience for them.

Stage three consists of helping and allowing the patient to experience separation and the end of a relationship in a healthy way. This concept will be discussed later in a section called *Saying Goodbye*.

CHAPTER IV

BIG CHANGES

I've seen a lot of changes in the practice of medicine and psychiatry in my fifty years of practice. In 1971, my first year, it felt like taking care of patients was a humanitarian effort. The focus was on people and their needs. I believed it was necessary to help those in need, whether they could pay my fee or not.

We treated people. Getting paid was almost an afterthought. Today, the focus is more business-oriented. The practice of medicine has changed from a humanitarian effort to an industry. We are no longer called doctors, but rather *providers*. We are providing a service, supposedly for the sake of patients. Yet lately I find that my attention needs to be directed at keeping out of trouble, such as malpractice claims. There are lawyers advertising to promise capital gains on any bad outcome. Then there are insurance companies flooding us with forms and questionnaires hoping to find ways to deny a claim.

When I started my practice in 1972 I did not need a secretary. I would see a patient and at the end of the visit they paid me. Simple. It was the patient's responsibility to deal with the health insurance system to get reimbursed, not mine. By the time I closed my office in 1997 thinking I would retire, I needed two full-time, and one part-time secretary. Oh, sorry – they are not called secretaries today; I meant "administrative assistants." My assistants spent most of their time with the complicated billing system so that it took more time to get paid than it took for me to earn the fee. One hour of my effort to help a patient required two or three hours of clerical work to get the reimbursement.

In the 1970s I would see a patient, jot down a note about the visit in the chart during the visit, and if needed, hand him a prescription. I could direct my efforts directly to the needs of my patient. Today I have to record the visit digitally in a computerized system after the visit. My attention is now directed at satisfying a dreaded audit. An audit is the health insurance company's effort to justify denial of my fee. The medications that may be needed by the patient are then e-mailed to a pharmacy. The recording of all this adds at least fifteen minutes of my time to the visit. In a typical day, that adds up to about two hours that used to be spent on the patient's needs.

The result of all this twaddle is that a typical patient chart has two or more pages of fiscal material for every page of medical information.

This has created a peculiar feeling for me in my treatment of patients. It is no longer a private, personal interaction between doctor and patient. It is more a feeling that the patient sitting there is only an incidental part of the huge system. The problems of the health insurance system are not the only intrusion on the patient's privacy.

A patient's emotional issue may have resulted from an injury. If they injured themselves at work, a worker's compensation lawyer may be involved and will need all the information in the patient's record. If the injury is not work related but has impaired the patient's ability to work, then his employer is now entitled to all the patient's personal problems.

So then there are health insurers, lawyers, and employers all busy destroying what used to be the almost sacred realm of the doctor-patient relationship.

CHAPTER V

THE MEDICAL MODEL

Prior to 1980 psychiatrists used the medical model. I have always thought that a "model" is a conceptualization of a problem that allows that problem to be addressed for solutions. The medical model then would be an approach to a patient's problem that would direct a means of correcting that problem. I would explain the medical model as having three parts. Part one is that there is a disruption of a tissue in some part of the body. Examples would be broken bone, a ruptured tendon, an ulcer in the stomach, which is a lesion of the stomach lining. Part two is that the disrupted tissue will cause symptoms that define a diagnosis. Part three is the diagnosis determines, or in medical parlance "indicates," a treatment with an expected result.

In psychiatry, there are major problems with this model. In the first place, we psychiatrists have never been able to determine what tissue, that is what material in the body, is disrupted, and where that tissue might be in order to explain or identify an illness. For years, the presumed tissue disruption had something to do with amines. Amines are chemicals produced by nerve cells and passed among those cells to create thoughts and behavior. When there is an excess or deficiency of these amines, symptoms such as abnormal thoughts, mood, and behavior, occur. One problem is that it isn't clear which amines are causing which thought, mood or behavior. Also, there are recent journal articles that suggest that these amines may be in the gastrointestinal system as well as in the brain. If all that isn't enough to destroy the first step of the medical model, the newest idea is that it may not be amines that are disrupted. The tissue disruption may be something called "TAAR." That means "Trace Amine Associated Reactors." Now any explanation of that is not only beyond the scope of this book, but it is beyond the scope of my understanding of it, let alone explaining it!

In the second step of the medical model, the tissue disruption will cause symptoms that can lead to a diagnosis. In psychiatry the "DSM" is supposed to help us do that. The "DSM" is the diagnostic and statistical manual with definitions and descriptions of all the mental illnesses. The trouble with this is the DSM often changes. It is now in its fifth edition and even that is being revised so there is a DSM-5R. Much more about the DSM is coming later.

CHAPTER VI

THE MEDICAL MODEL, CONTINUED

Now for the third part of the medical model, we need to consider that the diagnosis should determine, or indicate, a treatment. That may work in many of the medical and surgical specialties, but it is total fantasy in psychiatry!

The last time I opened a journal that promised to tell me the treatment of bipolar disorder, I was presented with six choices of medications and four augmentation strategies. Augmentation means adding another drug to make the first one work better. *(What?)* That means there would be twenty-four ways to treat the same disorder. But that is only the start of the quandary, because in my experience, if I apply any one of the twenty-four choices to ten patients, I will expect ten different results. The results I would expect would usually be the following: three patients will report "I'm better on this medication"; three will say something like "This medication didn't work"; three will say words to the effect that "This medication made me worse."

That leaves one more of the ten, and that would typically be the one that never even came back for an appointment. That patient looked up the medication on Google, and learned that it might cause weight gain. That patient of course did not want to risk gaining three or four pounds, even though he or she has beengoing through life with fifty or more pounds of excess weight. Damn! Those journal articles didn't warn me about that. The pharmaceutical representatives don't tell me these things either!

Then the question of which of these twenty-four choices is the best can be influenced by which drug company spends the most money on buying lunches for the entire treatment staff of the agency where the drug will be used.

No, the medical model does not work in psychiatry. The most I can hope for is the probability of helping a symptom or two with medication, and then deal with the social and personality problems of the patient.

CHAPTER VII

MAKING A DIAGNOSIS

I have always thought that there are two reasons to make a diagnosis. The first reason would be to determine a treatment. The diagnosis is supposed to be connected to a treatment choice. The second reason to make a diagnosis would be to communicate to others what you think the problem is.

By now I have seen that the connection between diagnosis and treatment may work very well in the medical and surgical specialties, but in psychiatry, it just doesn't. The last psychiatric journal article I read showed three new treatments for major depression. How am I supposed to trust that, when next month I will be likely be told that there are three treatments that are newer and better than the last three.

As for the second reason to make a diagnosis, it seems to me that counselors, and other people treating the patient, should know what disorder I am treating. It is also important that the health insurers know what they are paying for. The DSM (diagnostic and statistical manual) is supposed to help with this task. Any diagnosis in the DSM may precisely describe an illness, but in my experience patients never fit precisely into any of those illnesses. A recent patient provides a good example of this problem. He was referred to me following his discharge from a hospital with a diagnosis of bipolar disorder.

There are certain characteristics one might expect to find in the history of a patient with this diagnosis. For example, you would expect the person to have had periods of two or three months of hyperactivity and elevated mood alternating with periods of depression, with a likelihood of several months of remission in between. This patient had none of these. Rather, he had a history of chronic irritability, low stress tolerance, and a long history of relationship problems.

He was treated with mood-stabilizing medications. My guess is that his hospital caregivers wanted to treat what they saw – namely, irritability – so they gave him Lamictal, a mood stabilizer which is an appropriate medication for irritability. But since the treatment had to match the diagnosis, they had to use the diagnosis of bipolar disorder to placate the insurance company and to get paid. The patient was less irritable on the mood stabilizer and his overall function was better. He was not bipolar, though. He was chronically irritable. But prescribing mood stabilizers for irritability doesn't compute well with insurance companies. Hence, a bipolar diagnosis!

I have found a way around this problem. I use the diagnosis "Mood Disorder" for a wide variety of patient's problems. It has a code number of f39. The only meaning anyone can attribute to this diagnosis is "There is something wrong with this person's mood." So far, I have been able to use a wide variety of medications and treatments according to what symptoms or combination of symptoms I'm trying to correct.

There is more benefit to using this "mood disorder" diagnosis/code: Since it is a diagnosis that is quite imprecise, counselors and other people involved with this patient need more of an explanation of the person's problem. This way I can communicate useful information to co-workers on what the problem is that needs attention.

With the above-mentioned patient, being coded with a bipolar disorder would leave his counselor to think the problem was mainly a medication need. With the diagnosis of Mood Disorder I was able to confer with his counselor and deal with the patient's combination of biological and psychosocial problems. It was more of a team effort to help the patient's poor coping skills, his irritability, and especially his relationship dysfunction.

CHAPTER VIII

THE DSM

The Psychiatric Diagnostic and Statistical Manual – the DSM – a noble and scholarly work by leaders in the field of psychiatry, is an attempt to define and categorize all mental health problems. I use the term "problems" because the DSM does not identify illnesses per se. The problems defined in the DSM have been called "reactions" and in later editions have been referred to as "disorders." The first manual was published in 1952, with four more editions since. The most recent publication is a revision of the fifth edition.

Early in my career I considered the DSM a source of well-defined illnesses. I found that over the years the DSM became more difficult to use because the problems that people would present never fit well in those categories of illness defined in the DSM.

Here is a typical example. A forty-nine-year-old patient came to his first visit and reported depressed mood; diminished interest in usual activities; fatigue and loss of energy. That satisfied three of the nine symptoms listed in the DSM for a diagnosis of Major Depressive Episode. The DSM requires five of the nine symptoms to be met! In my opinion, he was depressed, plain and simple.

There is more. The five symptoms are only part of the requirement to establish the diagnosis of Major Depressive Disorder. The other requirements are that the five symptoms cause significant impairment in social or vocational function and the symptoms should not be attributable to substance abuse or medical conditions.

In my experience the likelihood of finding a person who is over fifty that isn't being treated for diabetes, hypertension, high cholesterol or some other possible mood-altering factor, is close to zero. Equally unlikely is trying to find a patient who is not using a little alcohol, cannabis, or medication.

In spite of these obstacles to satisfying the DSM criteria for major depression, I still have to try to help the patient who has only three of the required nine symptoms. I'm left with the need to treat symptoms even though the patient does not have a precisely defined illnesses. Now I have to figure out what to do with those five editions of the DSM on my bookcase!

CHAPTER IX

THE PATIENTS

Early in my career I realized that I would easily get distracted from the task of understanding my patient. Most patients would spend a lot of time talking about people in their lives. As a result, I would direct my attention to the people in their lives instead of directing my attention to the patient's needs. I would be learning more about the people in the patient's life than learning about the patient. For example at the end of a visit I would know more about the abusive husband than about the patient with me who was married to him. I might learn a lot about the difficult employer or co-workers than about the worker who was my patient.

A good example of this problem was seen in Mrs. X. She droned on forever about her husband's neglect and abuse. "He yells at me if I try to change the channel." "He spends more time with his friends than with me." "He never takes me out to eat." (That's strange. If two people go out to eat how can you know who is taking whom? Anyway!)

She painted a picture of a person I would come to dislike. Then I realized I was disliking a person I never met! I was learning more about a person in her life than I was learning about the patient I was supposed to help.

When I became aware of this distraction I began to see what was sitting right in front of me: a passive, compliant person who allowed the very condition she presented as her problem. Mrs X had no identity. She didn't even exist without someone telling her what to do or what they wanted from her. I saw the result of her passivity and compliance that she created even in me. I felt bored and even lonely with Mrs. X in the room, because there was nobody there. Her husband was more present in my mind than she. She could relate to me only in terms of her husband. She was setting up the same dynamic with me as she did with her husband. That is, she could be, or do, or think nothing unless someone told her what they needed from her. It looked like what Sullivan called "repetition compulsion."

Harry Stack Sullivan described repetition compulsion as the tendency some people have of setting up the very relationship of which they complain.

Whenever she talked about her husband, I saw the need to use the old psychiatric cliche, "How do you feel about that?" That didn't work so well though. Her response to "How did you feel about that?" would be a blank stare that almost said, "How am I supposed to feel?"

I thought of something more dramatic and more useful as a therapeutic intervention. I said to her, "If you keep talking about your husband, I'm going to get bored." Of course she continued on about her husband. I then faked a yawn and pretended to doze off. She, at first was shocked, and then realized it was a tactic and laughed about it. It worked! She began to see that she was not only boring in all her relationships, but also, she was setting up the very dynamic she was complaining about.

This was a good lesson in passivity and compliance. People with these traits can't affirm or establish their own needs, so they look to others for direction. That direction from others is often abusive. If not abusive, then another common outcome is abandonment.

The abandonment results when the partner of a passive compliant person becomes lonely and bored, and ends the relationship. The boredom result was what I tried to show Mrs. X by yawning.

She simply did not have enough of an identity to offer anyone company. She saw the problem. She saw that she needed to know her own feeling and her own needs and then make them known to the people in her life. After a few more visits with me she went home determined to declare her need to go out to eat with her husband. She chose the restaurant. She even drove with him in her car to emphasize the feeling of asserting her own need.

There was even a good lesson for me in this patient's experience. It was another example of the Sullivan method of providing a relationship experience for a patient that in Sullivan's words were "a corrective emotional experience."

CHAPTER X

ADDICTION

The word addiction generally brings to mind heroin, morphine, and the like. In my analysis there are two types of addiction: exogenous and endogenous. Exogenous refers to the addictions involving heroin et al. But for me the more interesting addictions are the endogenous; those are addictions to chemicals that are produced by the brain. I have little experience with, or knowledge of, exogenous addictions. I have always been fascinated by brain chemistry, ergo, my interest in endogenous addictions.

Both of these types of addictions have a common factor. They present a cycle of events. The starting point of the cycle is craving for a substance. Step two is the increase of craving to a point where thinking and judgement is altered, so that a good reason to satisfy the craving is created in the mind. Step three is the satisfaction of the craving. This is followed by step four, the remorse, and a promise to not use the substance again.

I saw step two in action once when I was a teenager. One of the kids in the neighborhood had sold his mother's drapes to get money to buy Valium. "Geo," I said, "you sold your mother's drapes?" His answer was a classic altered thinking of step two. "She never liked those drapes anyway." In step two of the cycle his thinking and judgement were altered to justify the satisfaction of his craving.

It's easy to see this cycle in exogenous addictions. The behavior is evident and the drug is obvious. Much more is known about these addictions, and much more is done about them in terms of treatment alternatives.

In endogenous addictions the four-step cycle is not so clear and often not even addressed as an illness. For example, for the obese patient, it might appear that the addiction is food. It's not. Rather, the substance craved is the endorphin substance made in the brain when the stomach is stretched. The obese person does not know about endorphins, but there is a craving for that relaxed feeling they get when endorphins are made in the brain. It is now known that there is a complex system of nerve connections from the stomach to the brain. There is a great deal of study and literature on this subject.

Richard Ambinder is one of many who have studied this subject.[1] He has demonstrated that when a person overeats, the brain is triggered to make and release endorphins, which are substances that act like morphine. An addiction is then highly likely.

Because of my interest in this cycle of behavior, I have made it a point to observe obese people when they dine in a restaurant. What I have noticed is good evidence of the addictive behavior cycle. Because of the craving for the addictive substance in the first step of the cycle, the obese person will eat fast and with little regard for flavor. They don't savor their food or drink, and don't even seem to be aware of the taste. They eat everything on their own plate and then look to see what is left on the plates of their companions in hope of eating what is left by them. When they have overeaten, the brain produces endorphins, the craving is satisfied and they appear more relaxed.

People who are overweight quite consistently show a comical example of stage two of the cycle of addictive behavior. They show a good example of denial by saying, "I don't eat much." I'm often left bewildered by how a person who weighs more than two hundred pounds can think they don't eat much. One time a student was in the room during a patient's visit. The patient weighed about two hundred and fifty pounds. I wrote the words, "I don't eat much" on a piece of paper. I asked the patient how much they ate in a day, and at the same time I showed the note to the student. As he was reading the note she was speaking the same words. The student was impressed by my skill. I could not take credit for it though, because there isn't much skill needed to predict an answer you have heard over a hundred times.

I believe the explanation as to how an obese person can think they don't eat much must be the difference between how much they eat and how much they would like to eat.

This pattern, or cycle, of behavior is obvious in the animal kingdom. When the stomach of a lion in the woods is empty he is in a "fight or flight" mode. There is much adrenalin flowing in his system. His pulse is increased and he is ready for action. When he catches his prey, he eats fast with little regard for flavor. When his stomach is full, he gets the "endorphin fix," he relaxes and usually goes to sleep.

A healthy example of this endogenous addiction cycle is seen in what is called "runner's high." In some people, running, or vigorous exercise, causes an endorphin production in the brain. The same cycle of behavior from craving to satisfaction and relaxation is evident. In "runner's high" though, step four is usually not present. There is no remorse, but rather more of a satisfaction and desire to run again.

I have witnessed a much less healthy example of this cycle in what is often called "the cutter." This refers to people who purposefully will cut themselves. It usually involves several razor cuts on the arm or leg. One time I asked one of my patients who had cut herself, "Why do you do that?" Her answer was, "I feel better." I know of only one way a cut of skin can cause a person to feel better, namely an "endorphin fix." It is that same connection of neurons that go from the stomach, the skin or other parts of the body to that place in the brain that produces endorphins.

An excess of tattoos may be another example of an endogenous addiction. I haven't seen many examples of this, but I recall an experience with two people, not patients, that I knew who had tattoos all over their bodies. I asked, "How do you feel when they are using those needles on you?" Their answer was a similar "I don't mind," and "not bad." I don't know of any studies on this, but my only explanation for how anyone could think that being poked with a needle over most of your body could be "not bad" has to be an addiction to brain-produced endorphins.

[1] *Richard Ambinder – Science News, 8/28/2017, p. 37*

CHAPTER XI

LONELY OR DEPRESSED

I have lost track of the number of times I have heard a patient with a chief complaint of depression followed by a perfect description of loneliness. There have been an extraordinary number of times that a patient has come to me with a history of treatment for bipolar or major affective disorder or other diagnoses that are supposed to be psychiatric, biological illnesses. They then give a history of social inadequacies, interpersonal dysfunction, and other problems leading to the real problem, loneliness.

I don't have exact numbers, but in my experience, a fair estimate would be that for every ten patients with a chief complaint of depression, two would have a biological illness; four would have a mixture of illnesses, and four would have a purely psychosocial problem of loneliness. It would also be likely that all ten of them would have a history of treatment with various medications.

Freud has offered a simple but ingenious way to differentiate depression and loneliness. He believed that loneliness is the feeling that something is missing in the world, while depression is the feeling that something is missing in the self. That is a useful and simple explanation of a distinction that is often ignored in clinical practice. It is also given little attention in psychiatric literature.

I have used Freud's idea in order to address the task of differentiating loneliness from depression. Depressed patients speak of symptoms, but lonely patients speak of situations. In the biological illness depression, the patient relates feelings of low self-worth, no energy or ambition, sleep and appetite changes, and other symptoms. The lonely patient, instead speaks of situations such as interpersonal conflicts, and the more common problem of the lack of interpersonal bonding.

Two of my supposed ten patients with the biological illness depression, usually respond very well to medications. The other eight end up in the treatment-resistant depression category; a category commonly known by its initials TRD. Google has hundreds of items under the heading "TRD in Psychiatry." Ironically a better term for these patients might be something like, "wrongly treated depression," since there is no medication that will fix loneliness!

Two examples of biological depression stand out in my memory. One was a 45-year-old dentist with no prior history of mental illness. He was successful in his dental practice and comfortable in his relationships with family and friends. He was an avid golfer. He came to me with a two-month onset of feelings of inadequacy in his work. He had begun to fear that he was not able to practice his craft adequately and needed reassurance from his wife. She worked with him and was available to give the reassurance he needed to continue a task. He would sometimes leave a patient in the middle of a dental procedure and go into the part of the office where his wife worked, and she would give him the reassurance he needed to finish the job. I prescribed an antidepressant, Imipramine, and in two weeks he returned to say that he was back to normal.

The second example was a doctor in general practice. He too was successful in his work and comfortable in his relationships with family and friends. He came to me with a month of worsening feelings of vulnerability. He felt that someone was about to pickpocket or mug him. The thoughts were intruding on his concentration. He too had a complete recovery after three weeks of Imipramine.

These two cases are typical of the biological illness of depression. It is a brain chemistry fault. There is an onset of symptoms in an otherwise well person. There is usually a good response to treatment with medications. Neither of the two patients were lonely. Both had good bonding with family, colleagues and friends. There was no need for counseling.

In any group of ten patients in my practice, I would expect only two of them would have illnesses similar to the above mentioned patients. Of the other eight, I would likely see that four of them would have a mixture of loneliness and a brain chemistry change that would justify the term depression. These would need counseling and might benefit from medication.

The remaining four patients would need assistance with their loneliness and interpersonal dysfunction. These are the people who often get treated wrongly with medications and end up in the "TRD" category. The other feature of this problem is that often lonely people are reluctant to admit it and come to doctors inappropriately seeking medication. The patient who denies his loneliness is often someone who will give a history that they live alone, they have no friends, and they have lost contact with all family members. I try to show this type of patient that idea that: to be alone and lonely is a problem, but to be alone and not lonely is a bigger problem! This doesn't go over so well because it's easier for the "lonely denier" to expect that a mediation will fix his problem.

One more type of loneliness should be considered. This is seen in the person who has had a life-long pattern of poor relationships. Most commonly it is the woman who has had two marriages with abusive men. She will declare that she has given up on trying to have a good relationship. She sees that life offers two choices: a bad relationship or no relationship. She ignores the possibility of a third choice: a good relationship.

CHAPTER XII

THE APPROACH-AVOIDANCE CONFLICT

In Psychology 101 I learned a fascinating interpersonal dynamic. It was called "The Approach-Avoidance Conflict." In the psychiatric literature, it is also known as "the Need-Fear Dilemma." I no longer have my psychology text book so I cannot remember the source, but the pictures that illustrate this concept are still vivid in my memory.

The idea was presented with three pictures each consisting of a donkey, a bale of hay, and a snake. Of course, one would expect that the donkey would be attracted to the hay, but fearful of the snake. In the first picture the donkey was equidistant between two separated bales of hay. The donkey couldn't move because he was drawn in opposite directions. This represented the Approach-Approach conflict.

In the second picture the donkey was equidistant between two separated snakes. Again, he couldn't move because he was repelled in opposite directions. This was the Avoidance-Avoidance conflict.

The third picture showed the snake and the hay together. Now the donkey was in an Approach-Avoidance conflict. He was attracted by the hay when at a distance from it, but repelled by the snake if and when he tried to approach the hay.

I have seen this dynamic countless times in my practice. Of course, I don't have much experience with donkeys! But time and again I have seen people unable to develop a relationship because of the Approach-Avoidance conflict. They need and fear the same object. They feel the need for a relationship and try to approach one. If they do try to risk having a closer relationship (approach), they feel a fear and need to back off (avoid) the feared object, which is that of a close relationship.

An example of this psychosocial problem brings to mind a patient I saw recently. Mr. X is a 51-year-old man with chronic interpersonal problems. He came to me unwillingly at the urging of his wife. She accompanied him and described his problem as one of extreme irritability. He agreed somewhat in that he said, "Sure, I blow up sometimes." But he said it with a peculiar attitude. It seemed he was defiant in a way, as if he thought he was entitled to this trait of an irritable tendency. His attitude seemed to communicate that he had a right to be this way and no one should criticize him for it. He didn't see that his irritability was a defense. He became irritable and drove people away when he felt anyone approach him with caring. I began to wonder why this woman had put up with this in their twenty-one-year marriage.

Then I began to use my interpersonal method of treatment. This meant I would see his belligerent attitude as the problem I needed to help him correct. The interpersonal method involves identifying the obstacles a person imposes on the natural evolution of caring and trust that is supposed to occur between humans. When this obstacle is identified, therapy is supposed to try to help the patient relate to the therapist without this trait. If the patient can relate to the therapist without his usual defense, then he is more likely to relate that way with others.

I began to understand why his wife stayed with him. She saw that he was lonely. I began to see it too.

Another part of the interpersonal method allows me to see my own feelings as having much to do with the person I'm relating to. I know how I feel when I am with someone who is lonely. I have always been a sucker for lonely people. They make me want to say, "Trust me, I'm on your side, I'm working for you."

I didn't do that on this first visit with Mr. X. It seemed to me that it would work better when he came back alone. My plan would be to try to gain enough of his trust to show him the interpersonal system that he is setting up in all his relationships. It is a typical "Approach-avoidance conflict" or "Need-fear dilemma." The system is seen in many lonely people. Their need, or loneliness, would make them approach relationships, but their fear of closeness makes them avoid any approach.

The result of this "Need-fear" problem in Mr. X and others with this dynamic is a curious stalemate. When he shows his lonely side, he invites his wife to approach. When she tries to approach, his irritability causes her to back away, and she is kept at a distance that he considers safe. This is repeated in all his relationships.

The conflict will be repeated in his relationship with me. The difference, hopefully, will be that when he applies the need or fear tactic, I will be able to show him that when I approach him with a caring attitude his irritability will drive me away. Then when I show a loss of caring, or a moving away attitude, he will then show his loneliness and need for caring, inviting me to approach him with a closer relationship.

The next step in this treatment process will be to help him identify the fear part of his dilemma. This is usually a fear of rejection based on his conviction that he is not worthy of the caring of anyone.

The fear of rejection that Mr. X had brings to my mind another important dynamic in relationships. I have seen it as a gigantic obstacle to the development of close relationships. My approach to helping patients with this problem involves trying to teach them that the basis for fear of rejection is connected to self-esteem. When a person has little or no self-esteem, when they think little of themselves, they see rejection as inevitable. It confirms what they believe: they are not worth caring about in a relationship. The confirmation is painful.

CHAPTER XIII

THE HISTRIONIC PERSONALITY

Today, there is a curious absence of a personality type that was common a decade ago. I am thinking of how often I would hear a female patient declare, "Men are no good. They only want one thing." I don't see much of this personality type anymore, and I haven't heard this complaint in more than ten years. The reason for its disappearance is complex, and may have more to do with social changes than psychiatry. Times and lifestyles have changed. The role of women in the workplace, sports, and media very likely has something to do with this change. The "Me Too" movement must figure into this change also, but I don't know how.

The patients that complained about men wanting only one thing usually were in a diagnostic category called "Histrionic Personality Disorder." One feature of this diagnosis, and the people who fit into it, is their need to be the center of attention. Women once satisfied this need by projecting sexiness. Of course, this results in men responding to what they see in these women: sexiness. Ironically, the one thing that men reacted to was often the only thing she had to offer.

About twenty years ago, when the "men are no good" idea was still prevalent, I had an unusual experience with one of these patients. She was in group therapy trying to correct her relationship problems. By diagnosis she was a Histrionic Personality Disorder. She was an attractive twenty-six-year-old. Typical of this type of patient, she sat in the group wearing tight fitted clothes revealing much of her sexuality. She was asked by one of the men in the group why she was still single. In a huff, she bleated, "I'm sick of men, they only want one thing."

There was a silence. I intervened. "Try this the next time you meet a man who only wants one thing. Tell him you know he wants sex, but that you will only have sex with him if you can give him one hundred dollars. See if he says 'No – I only want one thing.' " The group laughed. She didn't think it was funny, and she dropped out of treatment.

Of course there are attractive women who provoke sexual feelings in men, but are at least able to identify and welcome men who can offer a healthy, caring relationship. The patient who dropped out of our group was not this type. Typical of the histrionic personality, she could not trust, and lacked the insight needed to see and correct her trust problem.

Thinking back on that event, I now realized that the only explanation for why I could have allowed myself to use such an unorthodox "therapeutic" tactic was that I must have sensed that the times were changing. People were tired of such defenses, and it was getting difficult to take problems like hers seriously.

Also, I must have had in mind the message that men and women are not so different when it comes to what is offered to them. If sex is offered by dress, behavior, and attitude, it will be welcomed by whatever person is in need of it. If both money and sex are offered, they will be taken as eagerly, disproving the "men only want one thing" belief.

This patient was a common example of many women that I saw in the '50s and '60s. She had no vocational or athletic skills, no hobbies, and no interest in literature, politics or history. She spent most of her time shopping for clothes or getting her hair done.

By the '80s, this didn't work so well, since women had much more to offer than "one thing." Everyone is better for this. Why? Because as I look back at my fifty years of experience, I can see an extraordinary difference in the role of women in society, industry and politics. These changes are more a subject of sociology than what would fit in the memoir of a psychiatrist. But I can say that the personality type that is the basis of the "men only want one thing" attitude is long gone and not missed by anyone. Thankfully.

CHAPTER XIV

SLEEP

Have you ever wondered why there are so many TV ads for mattresses? In a typical commercial break you may see two or three ads for a medication, one or two ads for a law firm, and an ad for a mattress. Then there is the guy who wants you to believe you can't sleep because you don't have the right pillow!

I think I have the answer to this advertising jumble. The last ten patients I saw over fifty years old provided an interesting similarity and a possible explanation for the mattress ads. At least, in my experience.

All ten patients reported "sleep loss" with an onset of ten or more years, "and getting worse, doctor." There were two common factors that I noticed in the complaints. One was that the lack of sleep had no serious impact on their daytime function, whether at work or at leisure. The other more interesting factor was that all the patients spent between nine and ten hours in bed every night.

Scientific research shows that a person over fifty requires six or seven hours of sleep a day. In the textbook *Sleep Medicine,* the authors relate: "The basis for the age-dependent decline in sleep includes likely interactions between hypocretin and degradation of proteins, like B-amyloid, associated with neurodegeneration."[2]

Before anyone tries to digest that abstruse statement, it may be a relief to read that the authors add: "The ultimate significance of alterations in sleep with advancing years remains enigmatic."

My conclusion, after digesting this textbook information, is that older people need less sleep and it is usually in an interrupted pattern. A twenty year-old normally sleeps an uninterrupted eight hours. That changes with age. Therefore my ten patients are left with the feeling that they are not sleeping well because they spend nine hours in bed, but since they only need six hours of sleep, they believe that the three hours of awake time is sleep loss. They spend two or three hours every night worrying about why they can't sleep. Then a frequent compounding factor to this sleep loss complaint is that most people who make the complaint take a nap of an hour or more in the afternoon!

The complaint of "sleep loss" by a person over fifty should really be, "I'm not sleeping like I did when I was twenty."

So you may wonder why I started this topic with a mattress commercial. Because ... I'm watching to see if my ten patients will want a new mattress, or worse, will they fall for the scam by the "My Pillow" guy. I will be looking to block these wasteful measures.

I will also discourage the use of medications for patients who are trying to sleep as they did at age twenty. Most of those medications have consequences such as memory loss and the increased likelihood of falling. Instead of medications, I promote what I called "sleep hygiene": A list that includes: Establish a regular pattern of getting in and out of bed at the same time of day every day; Keep active during the day; Avoid daytime naps; Avoid watching TV while in bed.

I keep attentive to age-related sleep patterns and need for sleep hygiene because I feel the need to consider medical conditions that affect sleep. That text book *Sleep Medicine* describes sixteen different types of breathing problems in the category of "sleep apnea." There are ten different types of sleep disorders in the category called "movement disorders." There are also innumerable sleep problems secondary to medical and psychiatric illnesses. I had ruled out all these problems in my ten patients.

As for the mattress ads, I conclude that they are misleading. As for the pillow guy, he is an outright charlatan. He should get more sleep.

---

[2]*Principles and Practice of Sleep Medicine – M. Kryger, Thomas Roth, Philadelphia, PA. Elsevier, 2017*

CHAPTER XV

MORE ON CHANGES

I have already written about the change in psychiatric care from a humanitarian endeavor to an industry or business model. Now I have to address a bigger change that occurred in 1980. That was the year that the American Psychiatric Association foisted on psychiatrists a new model suggesting a new approach to the treatment of patients. It was called the "Biopsychosocial Model."

It was intended to show, or remind us, that the problems that patients complained of were a combination of biological, psychological and social factors. Biologic factors would include brain chemistry changes with an underlying genetic cause. Psychological factors would include personality traits, coping skills, attitudes, and dispositions that defined a person. Sociology would be the stress a patient was dealing with, such as problems with co-workers, marital conflict, acting-out children, and other interpersonal dysfunctions.

These were not new ideas. In 1930 Freud never wrote about biological factors in the problems his patients presented. Nothing was known about those factors at that time. He dealt with what he saw; psychology and sociology. He dealt with personality factors such as libido, ego and others. He also dealt with relationships as a factor of mental problems.

In 1960, psychiatrists became so excited about the benefits of all the new medications that were being discovered that they almost ignored the psychosocial factors. The journals were filled with studies about the benefits of pharmacology.

By 1980, it seemed to me that most psychiatrists were beginning to see the limitations of pharmacology in patient care. In meetings and lectures I attended, the main topic among psychiatrists was treating symptoms with medications. But more and more often someone in the meeting would remind us of the factors of social stress and coping abilities. It would usually be a counselor that would direct our attention to the psychosocial part of a patient's problem. The American Psychiatric Association saw this change also, because 1980 became the year in which the "Biopsychosocial Model" of psychiatry was introduced.

I have always been interested in dealing with patients' problems as the result of both biological and psychosocial factors. My problem was that the new model of 1980 would suggest that psychiatrists address biological factors only, and counselors would then deal with the psychosocial factors. As a psychiatrist, I would be expected to talk to patients about symptoms and what medication might help those symptoms. There would no longer be the traditional "fifty-minute hour" that psychiatrists once used. We would be expected to spend fifteen or twenty minutes with the patient who would leave with a prescription. The work stress, the marital conflict, the acting out child, or any other conflict would be the business of the counselors. All personal interaction between doctor and patient would be gone. It would feel as though I were trying to manipulate a computer program, instead of a brain.

I began to think that the new model might work if there were a lot of communication between doctor and counselor. But this didn't happen. I saw very little interaction between counselors and psychiatrists. When I call a counselor to discuss a patient, they are usually surprised at my attempt to understand the psychosocial problems of any patient. They are also relieved to be able to coordinate the care of patients with a partner. When I discuss a patient with another psychiatrist, it is rare that they know the name of the counselor the patient is seeing, and even more rare that they have coordinated the care of a patient with that counselor.

At the last meeting of psychiatrists I attended a patient was discussed in terms of diagnosis, symptoms and medication needed, and yet no one knew if the patient was in counseling. Nor did anyone know if the patient was working or was married. To me this looked like a total misuse of the intentions of the changes suggested in 1980. I thought we were supposed to see patients' problems as a combination of factors. Instead, the problems were separated into two specialties.

Sadly there is another way to look at all of this. That is, do we really need a specialty called psychiatry? Wow! Since neurologists are trained to address problems of brain chemistry, wouldn't it be more practical to have neurologists deal with the biological factors of psychiatric illness? Then counselors would deal with the psychosocial factors. *Uh-oh*, I'm talking myself out of a job.

CHAPTER XVI

I USE THE NEW MODEL

When I see a patient, whether it is a first visit or the hundredth, I ask a general question such as, "How are things?" or "What's going on in your life?" This usually directs me to which of the three components of emotional illness I need to address first. Of course I am mindful that all problems of patients will eventually be explained by a combination of biological, psychological and social factors – the BPS model. But my method, using a general question, usually draws out the most disturbing of the three factors.

The last ten patients I saw exhibited a distribution of the three components of illness, and that is quite common in my practice. Seven of them started the visit with complaints of social dysfunction. There were marital conflicts, work related stress and generally problems with other people, that is, social stress. Two of the ten reported psychological problems of poor stress tolerance, and that is most often based on lack of self-esteem, inability to trust, or fear of intimacy. These symptoms, or problems, are in the category of psychological stress. One of the ten showed a biological type of symptom, manifested by delusional thinking, paranoia and other distortions of unrealistic thinking.

Of course, even though the ten patients presented one of the three components of illness as the most salient problem and the main reason for the visit, eventually all patients showed the other two components. In my experience there is always an interaction of the three components in a "cause and effect" relationship. For example, an illness that changes brain chemistry – a biological factor – will have an impact on relationships – a social factor. In addition, social factors such as getting divorced, or getting fired from a job, can have an impact on brain chemistry.

The clinical pictures of my ten patients have much to do with where I work. It is a private enterprise. Therefore the patients need to be able to pay the costs of treatment with health insurance or cash co-payments. These patients have higher incomes which in many studies correlates with better mental health. The distribution would be much different if I were working in a psychiatric hospital or in one of the community mental health clinics funded by the federal government. In these facilities, the patients tend to present more severe levels of pathology.

So now, I have nine out of ten patients with mainly psychosocial problems and one of ten with an illness requiring medication in a medical biologic approach. If I follow the direction of the BPS model, they would have me refer nine of the ten patients to a counselor and I would be left with one!

I see the need to keep all ten patients, because I see an important role for me in treating patients with mainly psychosocial problems. That role includes the task of keeping these patients away from medications they think they need. That is a difficult task, because people come to me with an expectation that they need a medication, even for social conflicts! Of the nine patients previously mentioned, seven of them, when referred to me, were on a "Benzo." "Benzo" is a common term for benzodiazepine. This is a class of sedative, tranquilizing drugs such as Xanax, Valium, Klonopin, and others. These had been prescribed to the seven patients by the doctors and previous treating providers who referred these patients to me.

These drugs cause many problems. One problem is that they double the risk of falling in those over age fifty. Another problem caused by these drugs is that when used over a long period of time, they increase the loss of cognitive function. Memory and concentration abilities diminish.

If that isn't reason enough to avoid the long-term use of these drugs, an even worse problem caused by Benzos is that they block ability, or even the need, to cope with stress. A person using these drugs blunts the anxiety caused by stress, and they never learn to cope with that stress.

Standard and accepted use of Benzodiazepines are for temporary use in situations where a person's anxiety is blocking a necessary activity. The example I use to instruct patients of this is: If a patient works on the tenth floor of a building and has a phobia of elevators, then they will take the medication to get to work. Eventually that patient will be helped to gradually wean off the medication while learning to cope with the anxiety or phobia of the elevator.

My approach to the use of medications has always been: "Less is more." Ideally a person in good health should have no need for medication. Medications usually get in the way of the magnificent work of the brain in the production of chemicals. Melatonin is a good example. Melatonin is a chemical produced by the brain when darkness prevails. The patient who buys melatonin as a sleep aid needs to be told: "It's cheaper to let the brain make it." Taking it in pill form only blocks the brain from making it!

I discourage the use of melatonin for sleep or sedatives for chronic anxiety. That is easily justified since there are so many unhealthy consequences of these drugs.

It is not so easy to justify an attempt to discourage the use of medications in the antipsychotic category. These medications are usually needed to treat delusional thinking and hallucinations. But using them creates the need to deal with serious side effects.

Medications for psychosis often cause side effects of too much sedation, weight gain, and often many movement disorders.

I try to teach the patient to live with the symptoms and find ways to not let the symptoms intrude on function. Of course this isn't always possible if the hallucination is directing the patient to a dangerous activity. However not all hallucinations are dangerous. I have two patients which allow me to use the "less is more" idea and not prescribe for them. Both patients have symptoms of hearing voices that are critical of them. Both patients are well aware of the difference between the hallucinated voice and the vocal communication of people in the room. Since they know the difference, they are able to learn to ignore the hallucinated voice or just not let it bother them. Both of these patients were heavily medicated to block the hallucinations, and both had serious movement disorders and other side effects of sedation and libido problems. By means of encouraging them to learn to live with the hallucinations, both of these patients have been medication free for over a year. Of course, it has been necessary to monitor them closely, to make sure the hallucinations are critical of the patient only and not directive of any harmful behavior.

My approach to the new model is to minimize the pharmacologic treatments when possible, and continue to address the psychosocial factors bothering my patients. More importantly, I always address the psychosocial problems as a partnerwith the counselor of the patient.

CHAPTER XVII

SAYING GOODBYE

All relationships have to end. When they do, there are many results ranging from grief and denial to anger and sometimes even relief. The end of a relationship should be accompanied by sadness. By "should be," I don't mean to suggest that I make the rules; rather, the "should" refers to what is supposed to happen in healthy people with good bonding ability. In my practice, I have seen much less of healthy sadness to loss of a relationship than the troublesome reactions.

These reactions are usually presented by patients with a variety of intensities as well as in combinations. In order to deal with the various reactions to the end of a relationship, I have come to think about them in terms of the types of reactions I have labeled: the Graduation; the Breakup; the Funeral.

The Graduation

The category of relationship ending I call "the Graduation" is the least troubling in terms of patients discomfort or symptomatology. It may involve finishing high school or college. It also can include promotions at work, when the promotion involves relocation.

These are not usually reported as problems by patients. Sometimes these relationship endings involve some grief and some denial but not to the level of psychopathology in need of treatment. There are often tears at a graduation and more often the denial is in the form of one person saying, "Keep in touch now." The "keep in touch" gesture denies that the relationship is over. The denial gets in the way of feeling the sadness that would be the healthier reaction to the end of a relationship.

The graduation that I see most often in therapy is when a patient is better and believes, or needs to be told, that they no longer need treatment. There is often denial here also. The denial takes the form of the patient asking if they can come back if needed. I usually confront this denial, if it is denial, with a reminder that it's time to say goodbye. I try not to let the idea of coming back if needed, get in the way of the need to feel the healthy sadness of saying goodbye. Their thought of being able to come back to treatment if needed is an attempt to feel less of the sadness connected to the end of a relationship.

In group therapy one of the agreements I would require from a patient is that when they decide to leave therapy they will announce it to the group and then attend at least three more sessions. This sometimes gives them time to be confronted, if their reason for leaving the group is unrealistic. More often though, the three weeks will give them the much-needed and rarely experienced emotion of ending a relationship in a healthy way.

Another type of relationship ending in the "Graduation" category is an event called "Individuation." In psychiatric lexicon, individuation occurs when the relationship between a child and parent changes from the child's dependence, to the child's need to be his own person. This should occur when the child enters the teen years. For the parent, it is the end of a relationship with a child, and what should be the welcoming of a relationship with a new adult. In my practice I have often seen parents having a problem with the task of individuation. To a parent, usually a mother, the child's individuation means the mother loses her identity. Her sense of who she is will be gone if she can only see herself as a mother. If she lacks her own identity, her sense of self is overinvested in her child. In therapy, her task will be to let go of the mother role and find her own interests and her own identity.

The Breakup

The relationship end that I call "the Breakup" has been quite common in my practice. Often the breakup of a relationship is the reason for entering treatment. I have had an interesting realization when trying to help people with the hurt of a breakup. I have seen that there is a high degree of correlation between a person's self-esteem and the hurt they are suffering. The patients with little self-esteem suffer the most. To the person with little self-esteem the breakup, or "being dumped" confirms their belief that they are not worthy of the other person's caring.

On the other hand, those people who think a lot of themselves and have a lot of self-esteem, will see that the person who left them has a problem. The person with a lot of self-esteem will think, "How crazy they were to leave me and lose out on what they could have had."

The Funeral

The "Funeral" relationship end often provides an almost comical event. A funeral is a ritual created by most cultures to allow grieving and the need to say goodbye. This is rarely accomplished. At a funeral when someone begins to cry, there is often someone nearby that nudges them with an elbow while saying something like, "Pull yourself together, you have to be strong." Ironically that person is saying don't do what we came here to do! It is usually a man saying this to a woman. His real message is that her tears leave him with the feeling that he is supposed to make her feel better. Since he can't do anything about the death, he feels impotent. And the feeling of impotence is a terrible thing to give to most men!

I would encourage her to say to him: "I'm strong enough to show the world my sadness." Then she might want to show the "nudger" that he lacks that strength!

It is also strange how often I have seen a patient apologize for crying when it is a healthy expression of sadness. In this instance, I try to encourage them to see that there is no need to apologize. Then I try to show them that I am grateful for the trust they have in allowing me to be with them. Their tears are welcomed by me as an invitation to be with them in their usually private feelings.

Sometimes I remind a person that tearful expressions of sadness are quite different from whining. I see whining as an infantile attempt to manipulate. It's what kids do to get something they shouldn't have. Whining is the tearfulness at a funeral that is an attempt to get someone to make them feel better by taking away the sadness. That would be quite different from the healthy sadness that simply asks for solace and the need for company in the sadness.

There is one more relationship end that doesn't fit into any of the three categories. Every autumn many patients tell me that their depression is getting worse. Often the patient's mood disorder has been stable, but the autumn season change is difficult. When I encourage these patients to talk about the season, it frequently becomes evident that the holidays – Thanksgiving and Christmas – elicit sadness. I have seen that the older a person is, the more they feel the loss of family members. Holidays, for many, are a time to enjoy family relationships. My older patients can only regret the changes evidenced by that empty chair at the dinner table.

I have explained previously the need to understand the difference between depression and sadness. It is an important lesson on the road to healing.

CHAPTER XVIII

THE END

And now, the end is near, and so I face the final curtain! I'm only kidding, but I guess I did do it my way. All I can hope for now is that I have helped many and "at least did no harm." I often get reassurance that I have helped a lot of people. It's a small state and I often meet people I have treated when I am in a restaurant or at the mall. I usually don't remember them, but it feels good when they greet me and thank me for whatever benefit they feel they experienced.

In writing this, I can now see that the subjects and ideas I have dealt with here are most likely useful for counselors, nurse practitioners and maybe even psychiatry residents. I suppose I had these groups in mind when thinking about what I needed to say. But this treatise is also a practical guide for many who may not be in the medical field. And it is my personal statement; garnered after years of practice and thousands of patient encounters. It may be little more than a stepping stone that vaults you to do some research on your own. Or it may offer comfort in helping you understand you are not alone.

Wherever it takes you is where I want you to go.

I'm sure that many of the practices or tactics I have used over the years would be judged as right or wrong by others in the field of mental health. But I don't usually think in terms of right or wrong for anything. Rather, I make judgments based on results or consequences. If the result of an effort is good, that makes it right. The converse is equal. I learned this from a lawyer who surprised me when he said, "In law there is no right or wrong, but rather there is defensible or indefensible." He gave an example: The defendant said, "I shot the man in the chest." The lawyer asked, "Right or wrong?" That depends on more testimony. "I shot him because he was flirting with my wife": indefensible. "I shot him when he was coming at me with an axe raised in his hand, saying he would kill me": defensible.

This idea of "right or wrong" may be considered in my treatment of the two hallucinating patients I mentioned earlier. It is likely that many in this field would frown on the idea of not treating a hallucinating patient with antipsychotic medication. They would call it wrong. But those patients are better and have no bothersome side effects. Defensible!

In fifty years, "I did it my way" and the results were pretty good.

CITATIONS

[1]Richard Ambinder – Science News, 8/28/2017, p. 37

[2]Principles and Practice of Sleep Medicine – M. Kryger, Thomas Roth, Philadelphia, PA. Elsevier, 2017

ABOUT THE AUTHOR

John Ruggiano is a board-certified psychiatrist in his 49th year of practice. He grew up in Providence, Rhode Island. He received the Willard Achievement Award from his Alma Mater, Rhode Island College. He is the former Chief of Psychiatry at Rhode Island Hospital and former Assistant Professor of Psychiatry at Brown University. He now lives in Chepachet, Rhode Island with his wife Ellen Birkmann-Ruggiano, their three cats, and two rescue dogs.

www.ingramcontent.com/pod-product-compliance
Lightning Source LLC
LaVergne TN
LVHW020938090426
835512LV00020B/3408